Take a trip to
PANAMA

John Griffiths

Franklin Watts

London   New York   Sydney   Toronto

Facts about Panama

Area:
77,082 sq. km.
(29,762 sq. miles)

Population:
2,275,000 (1987)

Capital:
Panama City

Largest Cities:
Panama City (440,000)
Colón (69,000)

Official language:
Spanish

Religion:
Christianity (Roman
Catholics 89 per cent)

Main Exports:
Bananas, refined
petroleum, shrimps, sugar

Currency:
Balboa and U.S. dollar

Franklin Watts
96 Leonard Street
London EC2A 4RH

Franklin Watts Inc.
387 Park Avenue South
New York, N.Y. 10016

ISBN: UK Edition 0 86313 967 1
ISBN: US Edition 0-531-10736-1
Library of Congress Catalog Card No:
89-8929

© Franklin Watts Limited 1989

Typeset by Lineage, Watford
Printed in Hong Kong

Maps: Simon Roulstone
Design: K & Co

Front Cover: ZEFA
Back Cover: David Simson

Photographs: Andes Press 5, 8, 17, 26;
Stephen Benson 16, 18, 27, 31; J Allen
Cash 20, 22, 24, 28; Mary Evans 4;
Hutchinson Library 3, 7, 9, 21; Operation
Raleigh 25, 29; Remote Source 19; David
Simson 14; South American Pictures 6;
Frank Spooner 23; Survival Anglia 12,
13; ZEFA 15, 30.

Stamps: Chris Fairclough

The Republic of Panama is often called the "Bridge of the World", because it links North and South America. The Panama Canal, a waterway linking the Atlantic and Pacific Oceans, runs across the narrowest part of Panama. It is extremely important because of its location.

Panama was an important link between the two oceans even before the Canal was completed in 1914. Gold prospectors on their way to California in the 19th century, journeyed across Panama.

Most Panamanians are a mixture of peoples. Their ancestors include American Indians, the original inhabitants; Europeans, who came in the 16th century; and West Indians of African origin. The West Indians came to Panama in the early 20th century to work on the building of the canal.

The name Panama probably comes from an Indian word meaning "where fish are abundant". Such Indian groups as the Guayami, the Cuna, and the Choco still live in remote parts of the country. Spanish is the official language and most people are Roman Catholics.

6

Panama broke away from Spain in 1821. It became part of Colombia. Between 1850 and 1903 there were 50 uprisings. Independence was finally won in 1903. The construction of the Canal began four years later under the supervision of the United States. Panama still has many fine Spanish buildings.

The country contains a central spine of mountains. The mountains are at their highest at the frontier with Costa Rica. They become lower towards the Canal. The mountains rise again near the border with Colombia. The country possesses numerous rivers.

Forests, uncultivated land or swamps cover 85 per cent of Panama. Within the forests are found mighty, ancient hardwood trees, such as the valuable mahogany. Bananas and plantains grow along the coasts.

The picture shows some stamps and money used in Panama. The main unit of currency is the balboa, which is divided into 100 cents.

WORLD
MAP

PANAMA

Caribbean Sea

COSTA
RICA

Volcán
Barú ▲

Mosquitos
Gulf

Colón ●

Gatun
Lake

Panama
Canal

San Blas Mts

● Chepo

Panama
City

Tabasara Mts

● David

PANAMA

Santiago ●

Darién Mts

Puerto
Armuelles ●

Coiba
Island

Gulf of Panama

COLOMBIA

Pacific Ocean

11

Many parts of Panama are wild and remote. They provide sanctuary for a rich animal life. Animals from both North and South America, including pumas, ocelots, jaguars, javalis, tapirs (pictured), monkeys, and capybaras, rodents which can weigh up to 36 kg (80 lb), can all be found.

Hundreds of tropical birds and exotic flowers can be found in the forests. On the ground alligators and lizards and many kinds of poisonous snakes, fight for survival.

The country can be divided into five regions. The Darien region in the east is the largest. It makes up one-third of Panama and it consists largely of rain forests and swamps. The Central Isthmus is the 97 km (60-mile) strip between the Atlantic and Pacific oceans. It includes the canal.

Central Panama, to the southwest of the canal, contains most of the country's farmers and ranchers. Chiriqui the fourth region, is next to the Costa Rican border. The fifth region, called Atlantic Panama, is the source of bananas.

Panama is close to the equator. It has a hot and humid climate throughout the year. Heavy rainfall is followed by a dry season. All outdoor events are avoided during the rainy season. Professional baseball, and the country's golf tournament, are held in the dry season.

Spanish-speaking Panamanian men refer to themselves as Panameños. Men like to show how strong and daring they are, at the expense of women. This is called machismo.

At fiesta times, or on special occasions, Panamanian women wear the pollera, their national dress. The pollera consists of a loose blouse and skirt, made of a white fabric. It is elaborately decorated with flower, leaf, and bird design.

18

The population of Panama is concentrated between Panama City, the capital, and the Costa Rican border on the Pacific side. Few people live in the forests and swamps that stretch toward Colombia on the Atlantic side of the country.

Panama City and Colón, at either end of the Canal, are both thriving cities. They attract many tourists as well as Panamanians from the countryside. Both cities are crowded because many country people have arrived looking for work and a better life.

The government has tried to improve job opportunities and housing in rural areas. It is trying to improve the life of country people and slow down the movement of people into the overcrowded towns.

The Panama Canal is a marvel of engineering. It is nearly 82km (50.7 miles) long. With three locks at each end and the Gatun Lake, which is 26m (85 ft) above sea level, the Canal can be used by 90 per cent of the world's shipping.

Panama is a republic with an elected National Assembly. But the military play an important part in the government. The Commander-in-Chief of the Armed Forces, General Manuel Noriega, was accused of drug trafficking and the assassination of General Torrijos, Panama's ruler, in 1971.

The United States controlled the Panama Canal Zone until a 1979 treaty returned most of it to Panama. The treaty also allowed for Panama to take control of the canal itself from the year 2000. Another treaty gave the United States the right to defend the neutrality of the canal.

Education is compulsory from the age of 7 to 15. Until the 1970s, country areas were provided only with primary schools. All the secondary schools were in the towns. Education, as well as health, has improved in Panama since the 1960s, but there is still great room for improvement.

Panamanian music is joyful. It is a fusion of music from Spain, Central America, the West Indies, South America, and the United States. It is played with great enthusiasm at carnival time. The mejoraña and punto are the names given to the traditional music of Panama.

The most popular Panamanian dance is the tamborito, a dance that was popular in Spain in the 17th century. It was probably of African origin. The cumbia is Panama's other popular traditional dance. Both of these dances are performed during the fiestas of Holy Week.

Agriculture is largely confined to Central Panama, southwest of the Canal. It provides most of the country's needs. Rice, corn (maize), beans, root crops, bananas, coffee, cacao, sugar, and tobacco are all grown. Cattle are raised on small ranches.

Panama's rainforests are disappearing as poor farmers cut down trees and burn them for land. The removal of the trees is changing Panama's climate and reducing the amount of rainfall. This has lowered the water level in the Canal. By the year 2000, the Canal may be too shallow for some ships to use.

Panama is fortunate in being able to fish in two oceans, More than 50 kinds of fish and crustaceans of commercial use are caught. Fishing is an important part of the country's economy.

Panama's Indian people mined gold and silver before, and immediately after, the arrival of the Spanish. Now little other than rock salt is mined. As Panama prepares to take control of the canal, Panamanians hope to develop their economy and raise living standards.

Index